Henry Flanders

A Commemorative Address

delivered at the hall of the Historical society of Pennsylvania, November

10, 1844

Henry Flanders

A Commemorative Address
delivered at the hall of the Historical society of Pennsylvania, November 10, 1844

ISBN/EAN: 9783337386030

Printed in Europe, USA, Canada, Australia, Japan

Cover: Foto ©ninafisch / pixelio.de

More available books at **www.hansebooks.com**

A

COMMEMORATIVE ADDRESS

DELIVERED AT THE

HALL OF THE HISTORICAL SOCIETY OF PENNSYLVANIA,

November 10, 1884,

ON

JOHN WILLIAM WALLACE, LL.D.,

LATE PRESIDENT OF THE SOCIETY.

BY

Mr. HENRY FLANDERS.

PHILADELPHIA:
COLLINS PRINTING HOUSE, 705 JAYNE STREET.
1884.

INTRODUCTORY NOTE.

Mr. Wallace died on Saturday morning, January 12, 1884. A special meeting of the Council of the Historical Society was held on the afternoon of the Monday following, and his decease was announced to that body by its Chairman, the Hon. James T. Mitchell.

Upon motion of Mr. Charles R. Hildeburn the following resolutions were unanimously adopted :—

The Council of the Historical Society of Pennsylvania have heard with profound sorrow of the death of John William Wallace, who for the last fifteen years has presided over this Society with great ability and dignity. It is therefore fitting to give immediate expression to their sense of his services as an enthusiast in the cause of learning; of attainments as profound as they were varied; as a student of American history; as the Reporter of the law laid down by the highest court of the land; as an officer of this Society to whose interest the last years of his life were devoted; and as a man whose courteous manners and warm heart have endeared him to all.

Resolved, That in the death of John William Wallace, LL.D., this Society has suffered the loss of one to whose wise counsels, generous and constant benefactions, and unfailing interest in all its aims, it is most deeply indebted.

Resolved, That the members of the Council are painfully sensible of the loss of an associate whom they have long held in the highest esteem.

Resolved, That the Council will attend the funeral in a body.

Resolved, That the Society be recommended to take appropriate action at an early day, and that a copy of these resolutions be transmitted to the family.

A stated meeting of the Society was held upon the evening of the same day, Vice-President George de B. Keim in the chair, at which the above Resolutions of the Council were read.

Mr. Frederick D. Stone then moved that the Society approve the sentiments expressed in the resolutions of the Council, and that the following be entered upon the minutes of the Society:

The Historical Society of Pennsylvania, in the death of the Honorable John William Wallace LL.D., its late President, has met with a misfortune of exceeding severity. He was a gentleman of active and vigorous intellect, of the most extended culture, and the most varied attainments. He was imbued with an enthusiastic fondness for the cause of historical pursuits, and with a proper pride in the achievements of the people of Pennsylvania, and to his cultivated judgment, earnest efforts, and generous contributions, much of the development and prosperous growth of the Society is due.

Be it therefore Resolved, That the Council be requested to select an early day at which there shall be a suitable expression of our appreciation of the strength of character and merits of our late President, and of our acknowledgment of the many benefits he has conferred upon the Society.

This motion was seconded with appropriate remarks by the Hon. Horatio Gates Jones, and unanimously passed.

Upon motion of Mr. Hildeburn, it was resolved that when this meeting adjourns it will be to meet on Monday evening next, January 21.

Mr. Jones then moved that out of respect for the memory of Mr. Wallace, the meeting now adjourn without transacting any further business, and that the members of the Society attend his funeral at St. Peter's Church to-morrow, Tuesday, 15th inst., at eleven A. M.

A meeting of the Council was held February 6, 1884.

On motion of Mr. Carpenter, the Chairman was authorized to appoint a committee to take into consideration the subject of an address to be delivered before the Society as a memorial of the late President, Mr. Wallace, with power to act.

The committee appointed consisted of John Jordan, Jr., Samuel W. Pennypacker, and William Brooke Rawle, and at its request the following letter was addressed to Mr. Henry Flanders:—

HISTORICAL SOCIETY OF PENNSYLVANIA,
PHILADELPHIA, April 10, 1884.

DEAR SIR :

Shortly after the death of Mr. John William Wallace, The Historical Society of Pennsylvania directed its Council to make such arrangements that appropriate action should be taken by the Society in honor of the memory of its late President. The members of the special Committee of the Council, to which this matter was referred, have expressed their earnest wishes that you should deliver the memorial address, and on behalf of the Committee I have the honor to tender you an invitation to do so at such not too distant period as may suit your convenience.

Hoping to receive from you a favorable reply,

I remain very respectfully,

Your Obt. Servt.

WILLIAM BROOKE RAWLE.

HENRY FLANDERS, ESQ.

Mr. Flanders communicated his acceptance of this invitation to the Committee in the following words :—

PHILADELPHIA, April 12, 1884.

DEAR SIR :

In reply to your favor of the 10th inst., asking me on behalf of a special Committee of the Council of the Historical Society of Pennsylvania to deliver the memorial address in honor of Mr. John William Wallace, the late President of the Society, I beg to say that it will give me pleasure to comply with the wishes of your Committee.

I remain,

Very respectfully,

Your Obt. Servt.

HENRY FLANDERS.

WM. BROOKE RAWLE, ESQ.

The Address was delivered at the Hall of the Society on the evening of Nov. 10, 1884. A large number of ladies and gentlemen, members of the Society and friends of Mr. Wallace, were present. In the absence of the President, the Hon. Horatio Gates Jones, a Vice-President of the Society, presided.

After the speaker had concluded, Edward Shippen, M.D., U. S. N., arose and offered the following resolution :—

Resolved, That the thanks of the Society be extended to Mr. Flanders for his appropriate tribute to the memory of our late President, and that he be requested to furnish a copy of his address to the Society for publication.

This resolution was seconded with remarks by Ex-Governor the Hon. Henry M. Hoyt, and unanimously adopted.

The meeting then adjourned.

PRO PATRIA

John William Wallace

COMMEMORATIVE ADDRESS.

-

MR. PRESIDENT, LADIES AND GENTLEMEN:

JOHN WILLIAM WALLACE, the late President of the Historical Society of Pennsylvania, was born in Philadelphia, on the 17th day of February, 1815, and died in the city of his birth on the 12th day of January, 1884, in the 69th year of his age.

To those who believe that, following a physiological law, character, as well as physical qualities, is inheritable, and descends in a family from generation to generation, a brief sketch of Mr. Wallace's ancestry may not be uninteresting or inappropriate to this occasion.

The first of his line who came to this country was John Wallace, a son of the Rev. John Wallace of Drumellier, on the Tweed, Scotland, and Christian Murray, his wife, whose lineage, Mr. Burke, in his book on "Royal Descents," traces back to the royal family of Scotland.[1]

John Wallace settled at Newport, Rhode Island, in 1742, and several years after at Philadelphia.

He married here the daughter and only child of Joshua Maddox, a respected and honored citizen, a warden of Christ Church, a founder and one of the original Board of

[1] See Appendix.

2

Trustees of the University of Pennsylvania; and for a period of nineteen years a justice of the Court of Common Pleas.

John Wallace was a prosperous and successful merchant. He was too a man of literary tastes, and interested in public affairs. It is recorded on the monument that marks his last resting-place, in St. Peter's Church-yard, that he assisted to found the public library at Newport, since become the Redwood; that he was a founder of St. Andrew's Society in this city; and that from 1755 till the dissolution of the Royal Government in 1776 he was a councilman of the city. He died at his country seat, Hope Farm, New Jersey, September 26th, 1783.

His son, Joshua Maddox Wallace, after graduating at the University of Pennsylvania, was placed in a counting-house with a view to his pursuing a mercantile career. But his tastes for science and literature were stronger than for commerce, and marrying at an early age a daughter of Col. William Bradford, the patriot printer and soldier, he subsequently retired to his farm called Ellerslie, in Somerset County, New Jersey, and there and at Burlington passed the residue of his life. "He lived," writes the mother of our late president, "upon the income of a liberal inherited fortune, and in the exercise of conspicuous and unostentatious hospitality gathered around him the most distinguished men of the state and country." He did not, however, sink into the indolence of mere lettered ease, but was an active and energetic citizen. He was a member of the Convention of New Jersey that ratified the Constitution of the United States; a member of the Legislature of that State during the exciting political contests that grew out of the convulsions of the French Revolution ; a Trustee for many years of Princeton College ; a frequent delegate from the Diocese of New Jersey to the General Convention of the Episcopal Church ; and a Judge of the Pleas of Burlington County. He died at Burlington in 1819.

His son, John Bradford Wallace, was born at Ellerslie, his father's farm, August 17, 1778. He graduated at Princeton in 1794 at the early age of sixteen, and received the highest honors of his class. Designed for the law, he pursued his studies under the direction of his uncle, William Bradford, who was not more distinguished as a lawyer, and as the attorney-general of the United States in the administration of General Washington, than for those solid virtues and that well-compacted character which made him honored and beloved in life, and lamented in death.

Mr. Wallace was admitted to the bar, at Philadelphia, in 1799. It was a bar composed of very able and eminent men ; men whose fame, surviving the accidents of time, is still gratefully cherished by their successors. But in the shadow of these great names, such was the happy constitution of Mr. Wallace's mind, and so fully was it imbued with legal principles, and adorned with general culture, that he soon stood, not first perhaps, yet in the very first line of his profession. He pursued the practice of the law in this city with increasing honor and success until the year 1819. That was a year memorable for commercial disaster and distress. Many fortunes in that storm were swept away, and many families ruined. Mr. Wallace's elder brother, who was extensively engaged in foreign commerce, was one of the victims of the crisis, and Mr. Wallace was involved in the disastrous issue of his brother's affairs. Declining proffers of assistance from his friends, and equally declining compositions with his creditors, he set himself, with a stout heart, to the serious task of discharging the obligations which his brother's misfortunes had thrown upon him. Owning and controlling large tracts of land, hereditary and acquired, in the northwestern counties of Pennsylvania, he determined to remove to that region, and by his personal management and supervision endeavor to retrieve his fortunes. Accordingly, in 1822 Mr. Wallace left Philadelphia, and fixed his residence at Meadville, Crawford County. "This section of country," wrote Mrs. Wallace, in 1848, the year before her death, "now beautiful with cultivation, peopled with educated yeomanry, and everywhere marked by the institutions of civility and religion, was at that day signalized by the worst characteristics of democratic colonization." The track of the Indian, it is said, was then scarcely obliterated, and the primeval forest still skirted the streets of the town.

Into this region Mr. Wallace bore his courteous and dignified manners, his refined tastes, his cultured intellect, and his trained abilities as a lawyer. They won, as they could scarcely fail to win, recognition and respect, and secured to him as well the confidence and affection of the people among whom he lived. Although differing with him in political sentiment, the electors of Crawford sent him as their representative to successive legislatures, and until, triumphant over his pecuniary difficulties, he removed from Meadville, and resumed his residence in Philadelphia.

Mr. Wallace may, with truth, be said to have established the church of his faith, and of his fathers, in the north-western counties of Pennsylvania. "Conveying in his own hand probably the first prayer-book that made its way thither," says Mrs. Wallace, ... "he saw in a few years the ministry of his affections planted and established. His fiftieth birthday was fitly honored by the consecration of Christ Church, Meadville."

His endeavors and his abilities had led him out of the wilderness of pecuniary troubles, in which he had been compelled to wander, and with reviving fortune, in 1836, he returned to Philadelphia, here to spend the evening of his day. But he was not to realize the poet's aspiration and crown—

"A youth of labor with an age of ease."

In apparent perfect health, he suddenly, without premonition of the coming event, died on the seventh day of January, 1837, in the fifty-ninth year of his age.

Mr. Wallace married a sister of the late Horace Binney. She bore, without elation, his early successes, and shared, with a serene courage, his later adversities. Surviving him many years, she wrote, in the seventieth year of her age, a sketch of his life; a sketch marked by dignity and grace of expression, and breathing in every line the sincerest respect and affection. Her virtues, too, and her endowments of mind and character, have been delineated, and by a kindred hand. When she died at her country-house in Burlington,

New Jersey, on the eighth of July, in the year 1849, her
brother, Mr. Binney, sketched, not for the public eye, but in
his private journal, and, as he says, to gratify himself, and
assist his children's recollection of her, two or three of her
striking characteristics.

"My sister and myself," says Mr. Binney, "had probably
as strong an attachment to each other as brother and sister
have ever known. Both of us I think were deeply indebted
to the Giver of all good for vouchsafing both its strength
and continuance for so long a time. She was endued
with uncommon faculties and virtues, and adorned with fine
acquisitions both intellectual and external. I know of no
particular in which she was not to a remarkable degree
finished and accomplished. She would have become any
station from the highest which wears a coronet or sits upon
a throne, to the humblest to which is promised the King-
dom of Heaven. . . . From her earliest womanhood
to her death, she had the most uniformly and uninter-
ruptedly bright and vivid mind that I have ever personally
known in man or woman. I mean that at no time, in no
variation of her health or condition, for the term of fifty
years at least, did her mind appear to suffer the least sink-
ing or decline, the least obscuration or diminution of light
or lustre. I have never personally known any other man or
woman, however intellectual, whose mind was not occasion-
ally torpid or drowsy, as it were, on the wing, however able
generally to soar. I have often felt this myself; I mean a
drowsiness or torpor of the mind. But Mrs. Wallace's
mind was at all times, and in all states of health or spirits,

' wide awake,' not in the flashy sense of that expression,
which implies animal rather than intellectual vivacity, but
as a watchful and sleepless spirit that had all its ministers
about it, arrayed and alert for the service of the moment,
whatever it might be—action, defense, conversation, sympathy. Her intellect, to use the apt Bible word, was girded
about, and indeed it was a golden cincture, which diffused
light, while it supported and compacted together all her
faculties. . . . . Her spirit was oftentimes deeply
grieved by vicissitudes of fortune which filled her with
cruel apprehensions for those in whom she was bound up.
It was impossible to feel more acutely or to apprehend more
sensitively either the present or the contingent evils of such
vicissitudes. She had even deeper griefs than the loss of
fortune. She lost her husband, possessing and worthy of
all her love, at the first dawn of his reviving fortune, and
her oldest daughter in the maturity of her loveliness, when
the young mother and her first child were laid in the same
sepulchre. She lost several younger children. Her life
was anything but equal and cheerful; and her spirit in constant sympathy with her condition was sometimes bent to
the utmost, and though it remained unbroken, it never recov-
ered what the world calls cheerfulness. . . . . Yet
her intellect was ever and uniformly bright and vivid—ever
girded about with strength and truth—ever ready, even at the
very moment of suffering, to act and to serve, as if itself
were impassible. It seems to me as if no eclipse of fortune,
no cloud of adversity could dim for a moment the ethereal
rays that were shining there. And I must speak of another

of her characteristics, merely because it is so rare an adjunct to such accomplishments and acquirements as hers. She was totally destitute of vanity, and I believe never said or did anything in her life under such an impulse.

"In this mortal state, if nature has not so moulded us, and culture so expanded us as to dispose us to the love of others, and of other things, strongly and almost passionately, a brilliant mind may become a worshiper at its own shrine, and neither make nor allow any sacrifices but to self; and the heart may become half dead to other affections by the mere want of nutriment. So moulded and cultured from birth, Mrs. Wallace not only escaped this peril, but I never perceived that she was exposed to it. . . . At no time in my life did I discover that she had the least particle of vanity, or looked to her own distinction as the special end of anything she said or did. For many years before her death, her religious sentiments would have cast out such a motive as unbecoming her professions. But, in truth, I do not think it ever existed in her. She was no doubt conscious of her powers; she could not be otherwise. But she valued other things so much more than admiration, and embraced so many persons by her love, her family, her friends, her dependants, and sought and found her happiness in them to such a degree, that self was subordinated, and her heart became as much enlarged as her mind."

Thus did Mr. and Mrs. Wallace appear to the eye of kindred affection, and thus did they appear to observers not bound to them by any ties of blood. Mr. Webster, whose attention had been arrested by an article in one of the magazines from the polished pen of Horace Binney Wallace, wrote to him from the Senate chamber at Washington, under date of Feb. 4, 1848, and thus speaks of his parents: " With but only a slight personal acquaintance, I am yet not ignorant of your character, standing, and attainments; and you the more win my esteem from the affection which I entertained for your excellent father, and the fervor with which I cherish his memory. It is nearly thirty years since I first became the guest of your parents in Philadelphia. No house was ever more pleasant, no circle of acquaintance more agreeable than I found there. The remembrance of those times and those friends is dear to me. Your mother I am happy to hear enjoys good health, and all the happiness arising from the love and affection of good children, and the respect and kindness of all who know her."

The late Bishop Hopkins, in a letter to his son dated July 7, 1863, referring to his own labors in Western Pennsylvania, thus speaks of Mr. and Mrs. Wallace: " He was a very superior man, and a most zealous churchman, and the days in which we worked together at Meadville . . . . are still very fresh in my memory. Mrs. Wallace too was a rare union of remarkable cultivation, intellectual power, and deep piety, combined with a high refinement and untiring energy, which, on the whole, made up a character superior to any that I have seen in the qualities which secure a commanding influence in society."

Such were the parents of John William Wallace as described by their contemporaries. He was seven years old when they removed to the western wilderness, and a large

3

part of his boyhood was passed in that primeval scene. No doubt the advantages were greater than the disadvantages. Country air and country life impart a certain robustness of body and mind which the habitudes of the city are not so likely to confer. "It may be whimsical, but it is truth," says Goldsmith, "I have found by experience, that those who have spent all their lives in cities contract not only an effeminacy of habit, but even of thinking." Besides, he had before him, in his parents, the daily example of cultured manners, and his education was the object of their unremitted care and attention. He laid the foundation of his classical attainments under the guiding hand of his father, and in the same domestic school formed those excursive literary tastes, and those habits of study which distinguished him throughout his life. In his fifteenth year he entered the University of Pennsylvania, and graduated in the class of 1833. One of his classmates writes me, that at college he was "a marked individuality, and was held in high consideration for the extent of his knowledge on many subjects outside of the college course." These "outside subjects" so engaged his attention that "he did not work for or obtain the honors of his class, though all agreed," says his classmate, "that he could have had them had he chosen to try for them."

His college course ended, he was registered as a student in the office of his father, and in his father's office, and the office of Mr. John Sergeant, he completed his course of legal study. He was admitted to the bar of the Old District Court on the 27th day of October, 1836, and on January 30th, 1837, on motion of Mr. William M. Meredith, to the bar of the Common Pleas.

Mr. Wallace never actively engaged in the practice of his profession. His tastes did not incline him to the conflicts of the forum, and his circumstances did not compel him to engage in them. To most members of the profession the law is "a service and a livelihood;" to Mr. Wallace it was an abstract and liberal pursuit.

Throughout all his life, as has been truly said, he was a worker, not a dilettante legal trifler, but an earnest, accomplished, and useful worker. In 1842 he edited "Jebb's British Crown Cases Reserved," being cases reserved for consideration and decided by the Twelve Judges of England and Ireland, between the years 1822 and 1840. In 1841, having become the treasurer[1] and librarian[2] of the Law Association of Philadelphia, his attention was called to the comparative merits of the reports from the year books down. The result of his studies was a book upon the subject, a book upon the driest of themes, but which with his scholarship, his cultivated tastes, and quiet humor, is invested with

[1] He resigned the office of treasurer Dec. 3, 1864. In his letter of resignation he said : "Need I say that it is not without some emotion that I decline further election to an office which I have filled for nearly twenty-five years, a term of service longer than that of any other treasurer, and that I leave the office with a grateful sense of the confidence so long entertained towards me, and with my best wishes for one and for all of the numerous gentlemen with whom I have been so agreeably connected."

[2] He resigned the office of librarian Nov. 26, 1860, and in recognition of his services, the association conferred on him the appointment of honorary librarian, and the use of the library for life.

an interest that has challenged and held the attention of a wide circle of readers, and both in England and this country Wallace's " Reporters" has achieved high distinction, and is justly regarded as a legal classic.

As illustrating his treatment of his theme, I may be pardoned a single quotation. Speaking of Vernon's Reports, in the time of Charles II., he says : " It appears from the case of Atcherly *v.* Vernon, that Mr. Vernon's MSS, reports, found in his study after his death, were the subject of a suit in chancery between his widow, his residuary legatee, and the heir-at-law. The widow claimed them as included in the bequest ' of household goods and furniture ;' the trustees of the residuary estate regarded them as embraced by the expression, ' the residue of my personal estate ;' while the heir contended, that ' as *guardian of the reputation of his ancestor*' the MSS. belonged to him ; in the same way as would a right of action for the defacing of his ancestor's tomb. ' The printing or not printing of these papers,' says the counsel for the heir, ' may as much affect the reputation of Mr. Vernon as any monument or tomb. Possibly they are not fit to be printed ; possibly they were never intended to be printed.' ' Suppose a man of learning should have the misfortune to die in debt, can the creditors come into this court and pray a discovery of all his papers, that they may be printed for the payment of his debts ?'

" Lord Macclesfield, finding the decision difficult (and the parties probably thinking that it was doubtful), the dispute was arranged by the chancellor's keeping the MSS. himself; and under his direction, with that of Lord King, it was that they were first published. . . . . As it appeared, the heir had a good deal of weight in his arguments. The MSS. were not very 'fit to be printed,' and probably were 'never intended to be printed.' "

In 1844 Mr. Wallace was appointed standing master in chancery of the Supreme Court of Pennsylvania, and I am told by one of the most eminent equity lawyers at our bar, and who had occasion to appear before Mr. Wallace, in very important causes, that he discharged the duties of his semi-judicial position with zeal, learning, and ability.

In 1849 he undertook to report the decisions of the United States Circuit Court for this circuit, and three volumes of reports, known as Wallace Junior's Reports,[1] were the result of his labors. They are characterized by care in the statement of facts, and precision in the statement of the law. They have "none of the book-making scissor-work," said Judge Grier, "that disgraces so many of our books of reports."

In the spring of 1850, Mr. Wallace visited England. He went thither as the representative of the Law Association, "to visit the societies of Lincoln's and Gray's Inn and of the Temple in the city of London ; the Faculty of Advocates in the city of Edinburgh, and such other similar institutions abroad" as he might deem fit, and to report to the association how far the regulations "adopted by the wisdom of the bar of England through so many generations for the

[1] So called to distinguish them from his father's "Reports of Cases in the Circuit Court for the Third Circuit." The first edition of this latter work was published in 1801 ; the second in 1838.

preservation of its honor and interests," might be applicable to our younger and more popular institutions.

His mission and his letters of introduction gave him access to the highest circles of social and legal life. He made the acquaintance of Selwyn, Sir David Dundas, Mr. Sergeant Goulburn, and others of the bar; and the great lights of the bench, Lord Chief Justice Campbell, the Lord Chief Baron Pollock, and Sir Fitz Roy Kelly paid him marked attentions. Lord Campbell writes him a note under date of June 8, 1850, and says, "If you are at any time in the Court of Queen's Bench, I shall be much pleased to place you by my side, and to take your advice as my assessor." Mr. Wallace, it seems, accepted this invitation, for I find among his papers a letter (under date of June 20, 1850), from Mr. Sergeant Goulburn, in which he says: "I have been requested by Lord Campbell, whom I saw yesterday in Hyde Park, to express the pleasure it would give him if you were to repeat your visit to him on the Bench. He is now trying causes at Nisi Prius, some of them I doubt not of much interest. My elder brother also would be very glad if, when you return to your country and see Mr. Clay, you would remember him most kindly. He has a very lively recollection of that gentleman's worth and agreeable qualities whilst thrown with him at Ghent in the year 1814. Of course you will not fail to tell Peter how much I thank him for reminding me of him in so agreeable a manner by the introduction of yourself."

I may be pardoned for quoting one other letter, as a memento of Mr. Wallace's visit to England. It is from

Baron Pollock. "Accept my very sincere thanks," he says, "for your valuable present which I highly estimate, but chiefly as a memorial of your visit to this country, which has afforded me much pleasure. I have long desired to make such an acquaintance, and personally to know some members of the western branch of our great family, and I could not have had my wish gratified in a more agreeable manner than the occasion of your visit has fortunately presented. What history has recorded of our separation (which for the greatness of both nations and the happiness of mankind has taken place) may be forgotten like the differences between relatives in very early life, but there must always remain the common origin, the common language, the united literature, almost the same laws, and the same generous and noble objects; the advancement and improvement of the human race by the most free and liberal institutions. I am obliged by your kind offer, and beg in return to say, I shall feel grateful for an opportunity of showing to any friend of yours, how much pleasure your visit has given us, by doing everything in my power to render his sojourn here agreeable."[1]

While Mr. Wallace was gratifying his legal tastes and curiosity, and was aided in every way by his legal friends in attaining the objects of his mission, he saw at the same time a good deal of the higher social life of England through the attentions of the Earl of Carlisle, Lord Murray, and Lady Clavering. But he seems to have been most impressed by what he observed in the walks of his own profession,

---

[1] Dated June 21, 1850.

and "by those venerable colleges of the law" (The Inns of Court) "which," he writes, "through so many generations have kept the Bar of England together, not only with untarnished honor and elevated dignity, but in delightful fellowship, and with the sense, and in the power of unity."

The year following his visit to England, Mr. Wallace delivered a discourse before the Law Academy of Philadelphia, on *The Discrepancies of our Home Commercial Law*, and prefaced it with a charming description of one of the Inns of Court. As interesting in itself, and as illustrative of his style, I shall venture to make a quotation from it: "The Temple," he says, "is situated in the most ancient, populous, and busy part of London. If with us you should suppose a site—say from Market to Walnut Street, and sloping gently from Third Street to the edge of the Delaware, you would have some idea of the site of this Inn, in relation to the other parts of the city. Around the three sides of its site are built connectedly, and with more or less irregularity, the continuous structures which make the Temple. The outside, that is, the parts upon the street, are used for purposes of business; law booksellers, stationers, and other persons who supply the convenience of the Bar, being among the occupants. It is the inner part around and upon the square which constitutes the resort and abodes of the profession of England. Turning away from the mighty stream of business life which rolls by day and night along the strand, and entering through an archway that attracts no notice and reveals nothing within, you find yourself, after a short walk, within the Temple close. Here,

and in the neighboring Inns, is congregated the whole profession of England; and here every student must enter for
his education. Many lawyers and judges who are without
families, live here entirely, having a house or apartments
with offices and servants more or less expensive; living exactly as each man here does in the house he owns. Some
occupy 'chambers' only, or 'offices,' as we call them—
dining in the Temple Hall, where all students are obliged
to dine. In this place you find the *active* members of the
profession, whether leaders at Nisi Prius and the courts,
members of Parliament, of whom a great number are always
barristers, or the great law officers immediately connected
with the crown. Here also are those eminent *chamber
counsel* whose opinions settle half the concerns of London;
and those *law-writers*, perfectly known to the *profession*
everywhere, whose voices, however, are never heard in court,
nor their names within the 'city.' . . The Temple grounds, which break upon you when once within its
close, are beautiful. You are aware that the place was
many centuries ago the residence of the Knights Templars,
and like Fountains, Netley, Tintern, and other religious
houses in England, was selected and disposed by its founders
with comprehensive and exquisite taste. Before you lies
the Thames. On its opposite side, above, rise the time-
honored spires of Lambeth, and in greater distance the swell
of the Surrey Hills. The trees and walks and cloistered
gardens of the Temple impress you by their venerable
beauty, and the air of repose which they inspire to everything around. . Here is the Temple Church.

4

An idea of its beauty may be formed by the fact that
£70,000 have recently been expended in its repairs and deco-
ration. Its services are confined to the members of the Inn:
and being thus sustained by male voices only, have a monas-
tic and peculiar air. As the church comes down from the
religious order of Templars, it is said to be the only one in
London in which no child was ever baptized. . . .
In the Great Hall of the Middle Temple, a venerable structure with massive tables and benches that look as if they
had defied the wear of centuries, the members and students
of the Inn dine. The room is about sixty feet high. On
its richly stained windows you see the Armorial displays of
nearly two hundred of the great lawyers of ancient and
modern times, including among the latter, those of Lord
Cowper, Yorke, Somers, Kenyon, Alvanley, and Eldon. On
the wainscoted walls you have the names of the *Readers of
the Temple* for more than two centuries back: and portraits
of great benefactors. Here, too, the Bar assembles for occasions of state and festivity, and for ancient celebrations—
some very curious—which are still kept up with that instinct
of hereditation which belongs to no country but England.

" Everywhere about you, in short, in the names of avenues
and walks, in the designation of buildings, in the objects of
curiosity or interest or veneration, you have the names and
associations of the *law* before you. The profession is here in
its corporate dignity and impressiveness. It has about it all
those influences which Mr. Burke thought so valuable in the
structure of a state. It bears the impress of its name and
lineage, and inspires everywhere a consciousness of its

ancient and habitual dignity. The past is everywhere connected with the present, and you feel that the profession is an inheritance derived from forefathers, and to be transmitted to posterity."

In 1852 Mr. Wallace had the deep grief and misfortune to lose his gifted brother, Horace Binney Wallace; a grief and misfortune which were shared by all lovers of literature, and by all students and professors of the law. For he possessed a rare and radiant mind, which illumined every subject that engaged its attention. He had been one of the editors of Smith's Leading Cases in various branches of the law, and of White and Tudor's selection of Leading Cases in Equity; and of American Leading Cases in a diversified class of decisions. And he had shown in these labors a discrimination, a subtilty of thought, a power of analysis and reasoning, and a power of expression that were alike unusual and remarkable in a man of his years.

Upon the death of his brother, Mr. Wallace took his place in the editorship of two of these works, and Smith's Leading Cases and the American Leading Cases contain additional notes and references from his hand.

In 1857 Mr. Wallace again went abroad accompanied by his family,[1] and remained abroad until 1860. He passed most of these years on the Continent, residing chiefly at Rome and Florence. He had a cultivated taste, and a great love of the arts, painting, sculpture, and architecture; and

---

[1] Mr. Wallace married June 15, 1853, Miss Dorothea Francis Willing, a daughter of George Willing, Esq , of Philadelphia. The only child of this marriage is the wife of John Thompson Spencer. Esq., of the Philadelphia Bar.

he gratified and enlarged both his taste and knowledge by
studying them in their native air and home. His criticisms
upon these subjects, however, have never been printed, and
are not in that finished form that indicated on his part any
intention to give them to the press.

He had at all times a deep interest in ecclesiastical history; and the religious life of that ancient and venerable
church which for fifteen centuries was the bulwark and
only representative of Christianity in Western Europe, very
closely attracted, during his residence in Italy, his observa-
tion and study. But he was not alone interested in the
church in its outward and visible aspects, as it had appeared
on the theatre of history in the long succession of the ages,
but he had explored the foundations of the structure, and
made himself familiar with its dogmatic defences. Says one,
who was once his pastor and always his friend, " upon vital
questions touching the history, the discipline, and the doc-
trines of the church, but few even of the clergy of his day
could be said to have been more thoroughly furnished."[1]

Always a student and always engaged with law or letters, his life, in youth and age, was a life of busy occupation.
In 1863, he published a pamphlet on " Pennsylvania as
a Borrower." In this production, he considers the financial history of the State in the past, and points out what he
deems her true policy in the future. He reflects severely
on some passages of her financial legislation, but in doing
this he says : " I hope no reader will charge me with want
of loyalty to my State. I deny his right to consider himself,
in any particular or from any cause, more completely a

The Rev. W. W. Bronson

Pennsylvanian, however much worthier a one he may be, than I am."

On the 20th of May, in that year (1863), he delivered before the New York Historical Society the commemorative address on the two hundredth birthday of his ancestor, Mr. William Bradford, who introduced the art of printing into the Middle Colonies of British America. This address has all the characteristics of Mr. Wallace's literary labors, grace of style, and fulness of information and illustration. A stranger in reading it, said Bishop Odenheimer, might well ask, "How many professions hath Mr. Wallace studied? in which of the arts and sciences manifold hath he made greatest proficiency?" "It is," said Bishop Alonzo Potter, "a most graphic and lifelike picture of the olden time, and opens quite a new chapter of our early history. The typography is in admirable keeping with the subject and the occasion, and the whole forms a gem as unique as it is valuable." And our venerable historian Bancroft thus wrote in respect to it: "Accept my best thanks, dear Mr. Wallace, for your charming present. I like your address in the perusal still better than in the hearing; it is very interesting and exhaustive, in that best of taste which does full justice to a chosen subject, and avoids exaggeration."

While engaged in these literary pursuits, on the 21st of March, 1864, he was appointed the reporter of the Supreme Court of the United States. "On that day," he says,[1] "being in a very private station, and engaged in studies having but slight relation to the law, he was gratified, quite unexpectedly to himself, by an invitation from the Supreme Court

[1] Preface to vol. i. of Wallace's Reports.

of the United States to become the reporter of the decisions
of that tribunal. He repaired, with but little delay, to the
seat of government."

Mr. Wallace had very clear and definite views as to the
mode of preparing books of reports. It was a subject that
had engaged his reflections, and a subject too upon which
he had the light of his own experience to guide him. "Almost the first thing, therefore," he says, "after my reaching
Washington, was to seek an interview with each member
of the court, in relation to what I deemed a matter neces-
sary to be attended to in the style of reporting, and without
an attention to which I apprehend we can never have clean
and satisfactory reports. I was able, however, from the
lateness of my arrival in Washington prior to the adjourn-
ment and separating of the Court, to have less full confer-
ences with the judges on this matter than I could have
desired. Eight of the bench, as I understood, including the
Chief Justice, as I know, agreed with my views. 'You express exactly my ideas,' said Taney, C. J., 'as to the mode
in which the reports should be made. It is the only proper
mode. The case, arguments upon it (if the question is a
difficult one), and an opinion without a statement, is what
should appear in the published report, in whatever form the
opinion may have been heard from the bench.' Two judges
were of different opinions; their own. Certain of the reports,
therefore, are not in as clean a form as others."

Mr. Wallace held the position of reporter for a period of
twelve years. The labors of the Court during that time had
been vastly increased by the civil war; by the increase of our

population; by the growth of our railway system; by the multiplication of patents; by the extension of our domestic commerce; and by new and grave questions of constitutional law. All the varied cases arising out of these new and original sources, that came before the Court, many of them foreign to the system of law in which he had been educated, were most conscientiously studied by him, and each opinion of the Court was preceded by a carefully prepared statement of the facts, and the law of the case. Make any deductions you please for any faults of style or taste, which a friendly or unfriendly critic may perchance disclose, these twenty-three volumes of Wallace's Reports are nevertheless an invaluable legacy to the profession, and a memorial of the faithfulness and ability of the reporter. They constitute his monument and earthly fame. Monuments, indeed, perish. "There must be a period," says Lord Chief Justice Crewe, "and an end of all temporal things, *Finis rerum*, an end of names and dignities, and whatsoever is *terrene*," but so long as our Federal jurisprudence shall subsist and endure the name of John William Wallace will remain inscribed on the walls of its temples.

He resigned the office of reporter on the 9th of October, 1875.[1] In his letter of resignation, addressed to the Chief

---

[1] On the 3d of October, 1875, Mr. Wallace informed his publishers, the Messrs. Morrison, of his intended resignation of the office of reporter, in the following letter:—

"My Dear Morrisons:

I shall not come to Washington again. I am tired of such unintermitted labor as my office (much changed in this respect since I took it) now puts upon

Justice, he says: "I do not sever my relations with the Supreme Court, in which my term of labor, if not a long one, is perhaps hardly to be called short, without a measure of feeling. My prayer shall be for the Court; its stability, its harmony, its continuance in wisdom and learning, and for every blessing to all who belong to it." Upon receiving this letter, the Court made this order: "Ordered that the resignation by John William Wallace, Esq., of his office of reporter of the Court be accepted, to take effect upon the

me. I am tired of living half the year in a tavern; away from the society of my wife and child, and from the decencies of home. I am sixty years old, and crave independence from embarrassment by any one in what I see fit to do. It is not without some emotion that I put an end to my relations with the Federal city. I have made some acquaintances there which are among the most agreeable of my life. I have many recollections which, while my memory remains, will be pleasurable. I may say, however, with truth that I shall recall no persons with a more sincere regard than I shall always both of you; that I shall have no more pleasurable recollections than those of the many hours that I have spent where you were. In an intercourse of business running thro' twelve years, and embracing many transactions, there has never, once, been a question between us, nor one thought, I may venture, I am sure, to say for both of us, other than those of confidence and regard, between us. I have ever found you more ready to advance my interests than you seemed to be to advance your own; most obliging in every matter by which my convenience was to be promoted, and in the performance of engagements, prompt, cheerful, and liberal; faithful to the letter, true to the spirit. And all this intercourse has been the pleasantest imaginable; far from restraints and forms of any sort. Tho' we shall see each other no more as we have long done, I still hope not unfrequently to see you. I trust that neither of you will be in this city without letting me know. I shall certainly never be near Washington without coming to see you. Heaven guard, guide, and bless you both and all that concerns or which belongs to you! So prays, dear Morrisons, your affectionate friend.

JOHN WILLIAM WALLACE.

completion and publication of his twenty-second volume of
reports. And it is further ordered that when communicating to Mr. Wallace the fact of this acceptance, the Chief
Justice be requested to assure him, on behalf of the Court,
of their high appreciation as well of his uniform courtesy of
demeanor, as of the fidelity with which he has discharged
the duties of his office, and also to express to him their best
wishes for his future."

The Chief Justice, in communicating this action of the
Court to Mr. Wallace,[1] says: "We do all appreciate in the
highest degree the uniform courtesy and fidelity with which
you have performed the duties of your office during its many
years of patient labor, and you have from us, one and all,
the best of wishes for your future."

Mr. Wallace was elected a member of this Society, Nov.
24, 1844; one of its Vice-Presidents Feb. 8, 1864; and its
President April 13, 1868. From the time he became a
member of the Society he evinced a warm interest in its
objects, and availed himself of any opportunity that occurred
to serve it. When he became its President, though his
duties as reporter necessarily withdrew him for several
months of each year from the city, and absorbed much of
his time, he yet, at whatever cost of personal comfort or convenience, endeavored to be present at all of its important
meetings. And notwithstanding the labor which the preparation of his reports imposed on him, both during the
sessions of the court, and during the vacations, he yet com-

[1] The letter bears date Oct. 18, 1884.

5

posed and delivered before the Society a scholarly discourse, commemorative of the virtues and services of that distinguished churchman, the Rev. Benjamin Dorr, D.D.,[1] and a discourse on the inauguration of the new hall of the Society, at 820 Spruce Street; a discourse which recalls the history of the Society, and at the same time is replete with information, illustrating the annals of the city and State.[2] During the same period[3] he gave to the press a historical sketch of the corporation for the relief of the widows and children of clergymen of the Protestant Episcopal Church, under the title of " A Century of Beneficence, 1769–1869."

When he had resigned, and completed his work as reporter, his leisure was devoted to the affairs of this Society. In addition to MSS, books, and money, which at various times he gave with a liberal hand, the Society owes him much for his own personal labor and efforts to promote its interests. " He assisted personally," says the accomplished librarian of the Society, " in the arrangement of its manuscripts and pamphlets, and generously supplied many works which were needed in its collections. In our meetings he took an especial interest, and made it a point that every gentleman who was invited to address us should, if possible, be met with a full and appreciative audience. His presence as presiding officer upon such occasions could always be counted upon, and the dignity and ease with which he performed that office were sure to leave upon the minds of our guests pleasing and lasting impressions.

[1] Delivered Oct. 27, 1870.
[2] Delivered March 11, 1872.
[3] 1870.

Indeed, few who met him in our hall could fail to be struck with his kindness and attention, and his perfect manners. It was his constant aim to make the Society an institution commensurate with the importance of our State."

And, if it has, in some sort, attained to that proud position; if its material interests are on a safe foundation; if its historical treasures are rich and valuable; if its importance as a collector and preserver of historical memorials is now generally recognized and acknowledged, then, surely, for these large results, without disparagement to the generosity and labors of others, we may justly ascribe liberal praise to the generosity and labors of Mr. Wallace.

The last two years of his life were mainly devoted to the preparation of sketches of Col. William Bradford, the grandson of that William Bradford who, as we have already seen, introduced the art of printing into the Middle Colonies of British America. A limited edition of this work was printed, and only for presentation to his friends. But it is a most valuable memorial of the times in which Col. Bradford lived, and particularly interesting and instructive as to the history of our Revolutionary War. " The papers and manuscripts," says our librarian, " from which these sketches were prepared, he had arranged and bound for the Society in a style which a gentleman who has enjoyed the privilege of examining the manuscripts in the principal libraries of Europe denominated as princely."

In a little more than a month after presenting this volume to the Society, Mr. Wallace died, and was gathered unto his fathers.

And now having sketched the outward and visible labors of Mr. Wallace's laborious career, it remains to me to dwell for a few moments upon his general characteristics and qualities.

A lover of books; books, either in production or study, were the chief part of his life. He had a peculiar fondness for everything that relates not only to the inward grace of letters, but to what he termed their external charm. He had an accurate knowledge of the art, conservative of all the arts, the art of printing. No skilled and practical printer surpassed him in this sort of knowledge. A well-printed page and a well-bound book were a great attraction to him, and gave him a genuine pleasure.

His temperament was somewhat reserved, and he avoided, I think, general and promiscuous associations. But to those who came in close contact with him there was no reserve; and his powers of conversation, and his genial and humorous vein made him a delightful companion. He had enjoyed the acquaintance of many distinguished persons, and he imparted his recollections of men and things he had known and seen with a vivacity and freedom that were charming.

He was generous and charitable. But when he gave, either to public objects or to relieve and to make less onerous the burdens of private life, he did not sound a trumpet before him, nor let his left hand know what his right did. His charity sprang from a sense of duty, and not from any motive of ostentation.

He was a man of very positive likes and dislikes. And this extended as well to peoples and parties as to individuals.

He liked the Latin races, and he disliked the Teutonic races. He liked the Federal party, and he disliked the Democratic party. And although this latter feeling did not prevent or interrupt his friendship for individual Democrats, yet, I suspect, there was always an after-thought in his mind, that these unhappy people had inherited and were tainted with somewhat more of original sin than might otherwise have fallen to their lot.

There are in every country and every community two classes of men : the one looking to the past, and struggling to maintain the institutions, the modes of thought, and the habits of life inherited from the past ; the other looking to the future, intent on change, and hoping for progress and improvement. These conflicting classes keep the world, and particularly our modern world, in constant agitation, unrest, and discontent. Open war is, for the most part, averted by the so-called conservatives yielding their hold on some things, and by the so-called liberals sparing for a time other things, although in the end the stream flows on, however temporarily impeded in its course.

Mr. Wallace, from temperament, from association, from his habits of study and habits of life, stood in the ranks of the conservatives. He looked to the past rather than to the future.

Mr. Wallace was a sincere and devoted churchman. Modern speculations about man's evolution from some primal molecule, or some remote oyster, or some lively monkey, were foreign to all his habits of thought, and to all the instincts of his nature. He believed in God the Father

Almighty, Maker of heaven and earth, and of all things visible and invisible, and in the soul, and in immortality. And he lived and he died in the communion of the Catholic Church, and in the confidence of a certain faith.

The next volume of the Supreme Court Reports that appeared after Mr. Wallace's death very appropriately contained a brief sketch of his life. And it summed up his merits and accomplishments in these words, words which I conceive will be echoed by all those who knew him: "Mr. Wallace possessed a peculiar and charming cultivation; his acquaintance with history, biography, belles-lettres, and art was varied and exact, his conversation most attractive, and his old-time courtly manner, whether to the young or old, brought pleasure to both. Last and best, he was an upright, honored, and honorable man, and in public and private bore himself throughout as became an American gentleman."

APPENDIX.

(Extracted from "Royal Descents," etc. "By Sir Bernard Burke, LL.D., Ulster King of Arms," etc., ed. London, 1864.)

Wallace, of Philadelphia.

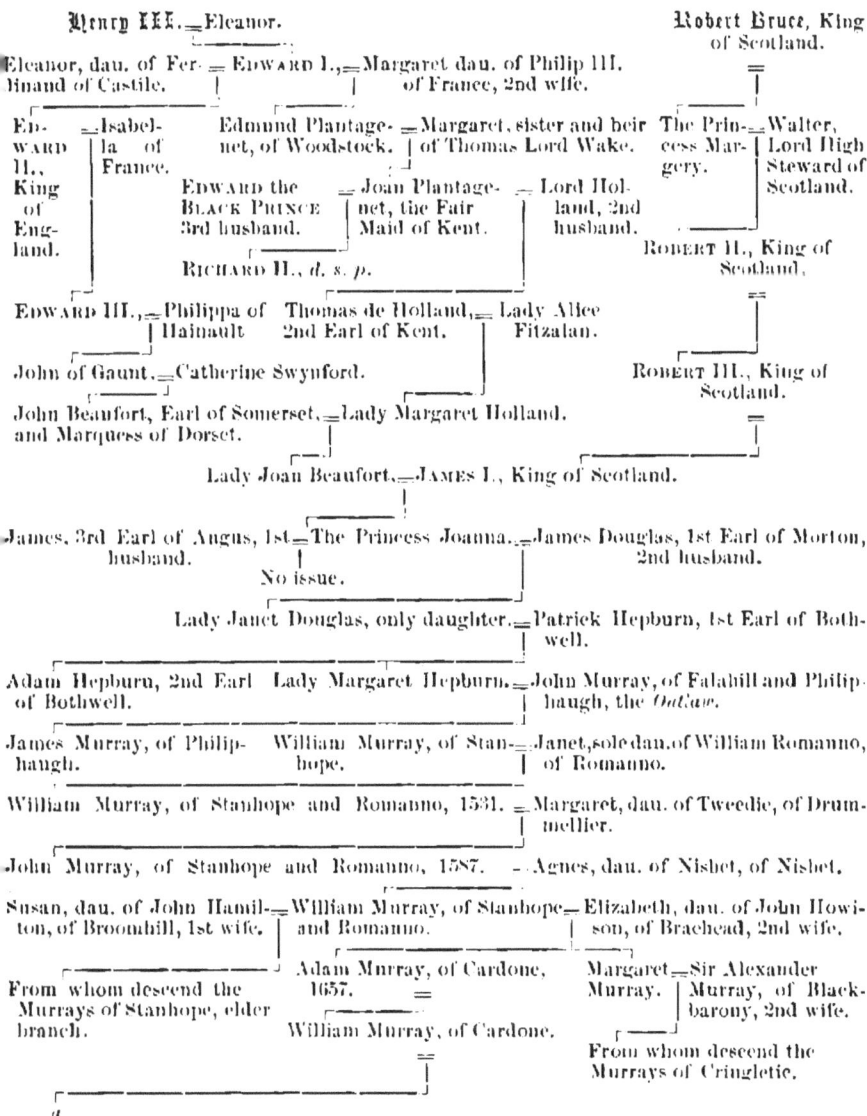

Henry III.—Eleanor.

Robert Bruce, King of Scotland.

Eleanor, dau. of Fer = Edward I.,—Margaret dau. of Philip III.
dinand of Castile. | of France, 2nd wife.

Ed- —Isabel- Edmund Plantage- —Margaret, sister and heir The Prin-—Walter,
ward la of net, of Woodstock. | of Thomas Lord Wake. cess Mar- | Lord High
II., France. gery. | Steward of
King Edward the — Joan Plantage- — Lord Hol- Scotland.
of Black Prince | net, the Fair land, 2nd
Eng- 3rd husband. | Maid of Kent. husband.
land. Robert II., King of
Richard II., d. s. p. Scotland.

Edward III.,—Philippa of Thomas de Holland,— Lady Alice
| Hainault 2nd Earl of Kent. | Fitzalan. Robert III., King of
John of Gaunt.—Catherine Swynford. Scotland.

John Beaufort, Earl of Somerset,—Lady Margaret Holland.
and Marquess of Dorset.

Lady Joan Beaufort,—James I., King of Scotland.

James, 3rd Earl of Angus, 1st—The Princess Joanna.—James Douglas, 1st Earl of Morton,
husband. | 2nd husband.
No issue.

Lady Janet Douglas, only daughter.—Patrick Hepburn, 1st Earl of Both-
| well.

Adam Hepburn, 2nd Earl Lady Margaret Hepburn.—John Murray, of Falahill and Philip-
of Bothwell. | haugh, the Outlaw.

James Murray, of Philip- William Murray, of Stan-—Janet, sole dau. of William Romanno,
haugh. hope. | of Romanno.

William Murray, of Stanhope and Romanno, 1531. —Margaret, dau. of Tweedie, of Drum-
| mellier.

John Murray, of Stanhope and Romanno, 1587. - Agnes, dau. of Nisbet, of Nisbet.

Susan, dau. of John Hamil-—William Murray, of Stanhope— Elizabeth, dau. of John Howi-
ton, of Broomhill, 1st wife. | and Romanno. | son, of Brachead, 2nd wife.

From whom descend the Adam Murray, of Cardone, Margaret—Sir Alexander
Murrays of Stanhope, elder 1657. Murray. | Murray, of Black-
branch. William Murray, of Cardone. | barony, 2nd wife.

From whom descend the
Murrays of Cringletie.

a

Christian Murray,* d. 21 Nov. 1755, aged 79 | Rev. John Wallace, Minister of Drumelliev.

John Wallace, of Hope Farm, Somerset County in New Jersey, Esq., b. at Drum melzier 7 Jan. 1718, went to America 1742. | Mary, sole dau. of the Hon. Joshua Maddox, Esq.

The Hon. Joshua Maddox Wallace, Esq., of Ellersbe and Burlington in Somerset County in New Jersey, b. 4 Oct. 1752, m. 1 Aug. 1775, d. 17 May, 1819. | Tace, dau. of Colonel William Bradford, of the American Army of 1776.

1. Joshua Maddox Wallace, Esq., b. 4 Sept. 1776, d. 7 Jan. 1821, m. in 1805, Rebecca, dau. of William McIlvaine, M.D.	John Bradford Wallace, Esq., of Philadelphia, Burlington, and Meadville, an eminent Barrister, b. 17 Aug. 1778, d. 7 Jan. 1837.	Susan, dau. of Barnabas Binney, M.D., a Surgeon in the American Army of 1776, m. 2 April 1805, d. 8 July, 1819.

1 Joshua Maddox Wallace, b. 1 Jan. 1815, d. 10 Nov. 1851.	Allee Lee, dau. of Wm. Shippen, M.D.	Other issue.	**John William Wallace, Esq.** of Philadelphia, only surviving son, b. 17 Feb. 1815.	Horace Binney, b. 27 Feb. 1817.	1. Susan Bradford, m. 16 June, 1841, Chas. Macalester, and d. 1842. 2. Mary Binney, m. 24 Nov. 1837, John Sims Riddle, and d. in 1852, leaving issue.

1. **William McIlvaine**, b. 28 Aug. 1818. 2. Shippen, b. 26 Feb. 1850. 3. Mary Cox, b. 25 Oct. 1851.

* Extract from the Register of Marriages in the Parish of Drumrnelzier, co. Peebles, Scotland.—"Mr John Wallace, Minister at Drummellier, and Christian Murray, lawful daughter to the deceased William Murray of Cardon."

See also Burke's "Peerage and Baronetage," pp. 720 and 721 (ed. 1851), and Burke's "Visitation of Seats and Arms," p. 51, and Plate XI. (2d Series, ed. 1854).

Note.—John William Wallace married Dorothea Francis, daughter of George Willing, Esq., of Philadelphia, and had issue Rebecca Blackwell Willing, who married John Thompson Spencer, of Maryland, and has issue Willing Harrison Spencer and Arthur Ringgold Spencer.

.

www.ingramcontent.com/pod-product-compliance
Lightning Source LLC
Chambersburg PA
CBHW021446090426
42739CB00009B/1661